AWAKENING

a poetic journey of Illumination

Dove Joy Grace

BookLeaf Publishing

India | USA | UK

Made with ❤ on the BookLeaf Publishing Platform
www.bookleafpub.in
www.bookleafpub.com

This book is dedicated to all the unseen souls who are struggling to reach New Earth and the higher dimensions. I see you. Keep going towards the Light while facing whatever comes up with forbearance and courage. You've got this. May this small offering illuminate your path and guide you on your way. We are One in Heart, and Many in Soul. Together, we rise into LOVE. Namaste.

Acknowledgement

I acknowledge Mother, Father, Goddess, God and all that is holy to be my soul source, my sole source. I acknowledge all of my families, birth, soul and otherwise. They have been some of my greatest teachers, ever keeping me humble and heading toward the light. And most of all, I acknowledge Love. We are One in Spirit, many in Soul. One in Heart, many in Mind. May we all learn to work and play and love and grow together in Harmony, Goodwill and Peace. With the light of Joy leading the way.

Preface

This book has been 30 years in the making. It is part of a collection of channeled material I received from Spirit in 1989 and 1990 in answer to my cries for healing from years of abuse and bad choices. The words and ideas presented here have carried me forward on a spiritual journey that has been breathtaking in its scope.

The poems themselves disappeared into storage for most of that 30 years. They came to light again during the pandemic in an extraordinary way. Once more, in answer to my prayer to reconnect with the material buried in the closet. A friend had reminded me of New Genesis and asked for a copy.

Two days after I asked for the New Genesis to reappear with ease, grace and joy, it certainly did.

I walked into my art room/office and there on the floor was one of my boxes I could swear had been in the closet.

Spilling out of it was pure golden treasure that I now humbly share with you. From my heart and soul to yours.

Love,
Dove Joy Grace

New Genesis

"And the deserts shall bloom
Dead trees will again bear fruit
Dry wells will spring anew
Overflowing with the abundance
Of the Holy Breath made manifest."

The parched souls of men will find
refreshment at the waterfall
Fruit and honey will fill the emptiness inside
Cool breezes will soothe the fevered brow
And the hearts of women will again grow
glad
Freed at last, from the bondage of separation.

Armageddon destroys only itself.
The demons will at last be put to rest
The might of Love will rear up, unafraid
And smote as a feather
oppression at its root.

And the heart shall blossom, ever gently in
the sun
Whose rays will at last be tempered

And burn no more.
The rain, in its place, shall come with its
assistance
To wash away the remnants and pain no more
shall be.

And the Holiness within will at last be
released
As the tide rushes in, men's hearts and
women's minds
Will be free to embrace a Golden New Day.

A new vision forms on the horizon of Time
Cleansed and free where all are made One
And Harmony reigns.

And the swords become as feathers
The hearts of all rejoice.
Oppression rules no more
Body's role is at last understood
and the path of Grace is revealed.

The splendor and beauty
that adorn the Holy Face
Shall be seen for what it is.
At last the mirror sees itself rightly

And joy replaces scorn forevermore.

The Holy Breath breathes lightly
Grace shines its light divine
The Holy Form made manifest
Becomes a fountain of Love.

All walls will take their proper place
Against the evil ways of oppression's
ignorance
that darkness reigns no more.

The Earth will be redeemed in the hearts and
eyes of all
True Honor will flourish
And each will find their way in joy and
gladness
springing from the wellspring in the breast
The bounty of Heaven will at last be manifest.

The Word of God incarnate is what we are
And evermore shall be
When once this truth takes hold in all
The garden's fruits will come again
And winter will no more be.

For we are meant to live in fullness
Bounty's feast is here for All
God's blessings know no limitations and this
understanding
brings relief of past misunderstandings.

Which is all the chains that bind us are.
No more will ghosts and goblins haunt us
As we awake from slumber deep
The nightmare is ended
Reality is dawning
Humanity's rebirthday is coming
The labor has begun.

As the threshold is cross'd fear grips the heart
but does not have to hinder, for it is written
and inevitable
That Birth is here again.

Each one must make a choice to struggle
or surrender
For free will is the only law
that cannot be transgressed.

Each one may choose the ease of birth

The secret lies at death's door
The harder one resists this Time
The more arduous the path becomes.

Indeed some will be stillborn
But the tide of humanity will not be stopped
And all who choose to embrace the New Day
will be guided and aided by the midwives of
compassion
Seen and unseen, available to all who call for
assistance.

Angels are amongst the world
And master spirits abound in flesh
For we of Heaven and you of Earth
Together build the bridge over which
The Miracle manifests.

For this indeed is what takes place
A bridge of Light is built
Between the realms of Spirit and Flesh
That each may know the other and embrace
in divine and holy matrimony.

Nevermore again to be divided
The prodigal way at last is ending
The lessons of suffering are complete.
Compassion's flame burns brightly
Lighting up the heavens for all to see.

And the Body of Light will then rise
To spread the light divine
To all corners where darkness dwells
And ignite the torch of Love.

Into Eternity the Body will travel
Forevermore One with
FatherMother God of Gods
Seeding new civilizations of light and love
Where no more will lessons of suffering be
necessary.

For once and for all
The cleansing is Now, nevermore to come
again.
For once the next cycle's dawn is come
Understanding's light will ease the way
And delivery's aim will be fulfilled
in total joy and absolute surrender.

ANGEL OF HOPE

The Path

The in-dwelling presence of the One
is the golden goal for all.
Jesus, Buddha, the Dali Lama
and all the teachers of the world
are simply that.
Teachers.
They have each found their path
to the in-dwelling Place
The Holy Temple of the Heart
the true home of heaven.

Each one must take responsibility
to seek the path
 that vibrates with them.
It may be one only they tread upon.
The path chosen does not matter
They all lead to the same place:
Reunion with our Creator.

When once this place is found in each
Heaven cannot be kept from blossoming
forth
upon our beloved planet

For it is what is seen with the heart
that brings outer experience
Appearance reality is simply the draping
of the energy within.

Whilst one is lost and forlorn
the outer reflection can bring only that.
Whilst envy, greed, hatred rule the mind
they will continue to plague the Earth.

Conversely, once the mind and heart are
redirected
to the in-dwelling Holiness
Nothing can stop the rushing forward
Of the Divine Destiny to our outer reality.

Unity Requires Us All

We mend the Sacred Hoop by sharing
Our Truths.
Take responsibility for your part
in the Healing
of the WHOLE.

Support the strength.
Forgive
the
weakness.

Until Now

Eternity: a concept too vast
until now.
Vulnerability: too risky
until now.
Since we've met I've begun to be aware of
Outmoded definitions that have limited me
imprisoned me without my even knowing.
The shell of fear, the bars of judgment that
have colored my life mottled
until now.
Suddenly, new depths, new realities have
entered
rendering me breathless from their sheer
beauty
Awestruck by their profundity
Humbled by the easy grace with which they
arrived.
I thought I'd known love before.
Finally I understand.
Love cannot be known.
Only honored.

Dark Night

Rent asunder
Lost
amidst the whitecaps in the storm of our
Being
peaks and valleys that separate us from
ourselves.
times of healing require strength.
Solitude beckons as issues overwhelm
our senses.
Fear sickens us as the walls of self-made
prisons of judgment
compress further.
In these times of testing beyond measure
the God-within ignites
the flame flickers, wavers;
despair grows thicker.
But just as endurance runs out
and the pain of holding on becomes
unbearable
The Light within takes hold and begins to
capture us

warm and comfort us
until all struggle ceases
And we find our solutions in surrender and
release.

Uncovering Truth

Reality is not the events of our lives
themselves
But rather,
the energy underlying.
Never are we permitted to look directly into
Her Face.
Only reflections are ours to perceive:
myriad, kaleidoscopic
Speeding up and slowing down
with the rhythm of our personal melody.
We fully determine the beauty thereof
By depth
of perception.

Subtle Beginnings

Change in an instant.
One look, one touch
Unexpectedly the heart opens tenuously
Embracing a deeper connection:
Freedom's pipeline.
How long unnoticed,
Unseen in the winter of the soul
Have these seeds been lying seemingly
dormant?
Yet, one day, in comfortable innocence
Eyes meet
A new light dawns
Destiny is fulfilled.

The Other Day

The other day something new was born
between us
Friendly banter gained an intimate edge
Casual touches grew more frequent
Tenderness entered the air around us
Our eyes unexpectedly caressed each other
Quietly awakening a long-slumbering love.
The other day.

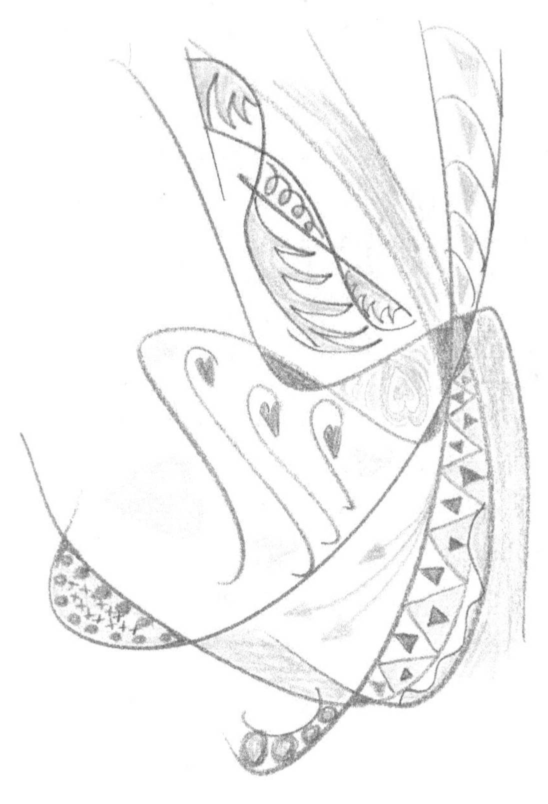

AWAKENING

Exploration

In wholeness we celebrate new beginnings.
As-yet unexplored possibilities lie between us
Beckoning gently, calling softly to be fulfilled.
Images of you dance before my eyes
Quickening my heart with upsurgings of joy.
A new way of loving is drawn in with each
breath.
We have merged in Spirit immutably now.
All separation is dissolved
Bringing a new dimension of freedom felt at
my core
Releasing all need to control or direct.
All that remains is reverence for the
experience.

Dilemma

How do we know when to let go?
When the lesson's completed the signs are all
there.
Yet we loathe to heed, fearing...
What?
The "unknown as enemy" is really the shackle
That needs befriending.
Without the unknown
Life is a computer.

Finding Love

Always before have I sought reassurance
Hungered for acceptance
Longed for understanding, thirsted for love
Outside of myself.
Loving myself never seemed good enough
Outer validation was my unquenchable
craving.
Slowly, as I peel back the pain, chip away at
the encrustations
Of fear and guilt, rage and shame
I have begun to ask why do I feel so
unworthy?
A beggar at a banquet, starving yet
immobilized.
Step by step I'm learning to see and
beginning to feel
The Real Self within is the Keeper of Love
and lives
Underneath the trappings of death.
All we need to do is build a bridge between
the inner and outer
To find enduring Love and true Fulfillment.

Stuck in the Mind?

Why is it so difficult to bridge the intellect
and emotions?
Continually opposed, it seems
sapping our energy, tearing us in two.
The mind wields its mighty logic like a
weapon
overpowering the tender heart
oppressive in its judgment
insanity-producing in its ability
to confuse and appear right.
whereas the heart is simple, pure, direct.
When allowed to flow unencumbered
free of judgment, cleansed of pain
It will guide us unerringly with the light of its
love.
the mind has no regard for any but itself.
If only it could learn humility.
Learn to listen to and respect the views of the
Heart.
Learn that its true function is valuable
but severely limited.
Learn that without the Heart, the mind only
creates death

then, and only then
Will Unity be achieved and
Harmony and Wisdom will reign.

Limitless Love

When we are centered securely, serenely in
our multi-dimensionality.
All limitations fall away
dissolve as quickly, as unceremoniously
as snow in July.
Leaving us in shimmering Reality
Illuminated by the knowledge that
Each moment contains an infinity of choice.
Experiencing all faces of love with the One
creates the Dance of Eternity.

Unchanging Changefull-ness

The heart's knowing is stillness in movement
Honoring changefull-ness without censure
Requires surrender without question
And brings the resolution of the Paradox of
Duality.

Real Love

Real love does not guarantee tomorrow's
expression
It lives for the Eternal Today.
It does not offer security
But rather, brings excitement to the unknown
The only way to find it is to risk losing all.

The Secret Weapon

The hardest of all to bear is humiliation,
degradation and scorn
When dignity is lost, the battle endangers us
The secret weapon is to fully grasp the
knowledge
That dignity is a state of HEART
Which is within our ability to maintain under
attack
This is the core of invincibility.

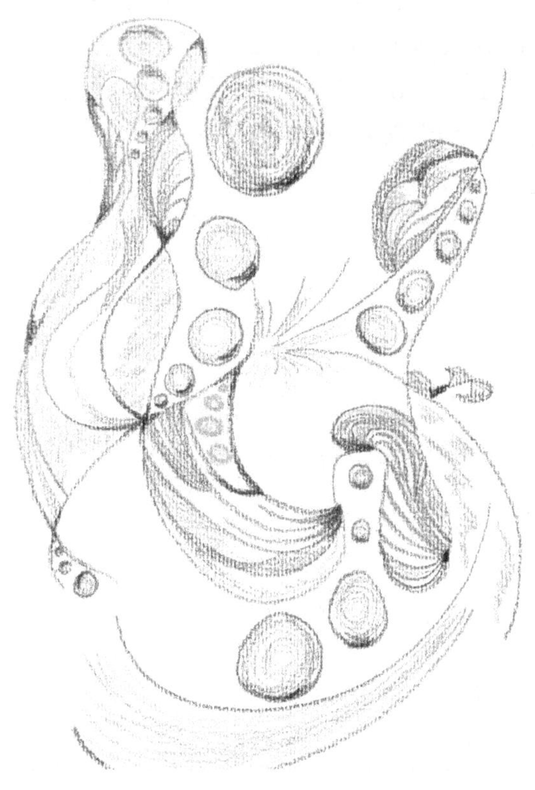

TWIN FLAMES

Goodbye dis-ease

The time has come at last to bid farewell
To the arsenal of the past
No longer do self-attack, -blame, -hatred
Have a place in my being
Goodbye dis-ease
Hello Love.

Darkness into Light

Cruelty embodies unconsciousness
When brought to Light
Its power dissolves with understanding.

The Way Out

At the core of victimhood is a shroud of guilt
so thick
It stifles the soul's expression
A desire for punishment that is relentless in
its brutality
Merciless, death-oriented
Rendering the heart desperate, immobilized
by terror.
Uprooting the judgments one by one
The "sins" of the soul, both real and imagined
All must be seen, claimed and forgiven.
The way out.

When the Muse Speaks

Touching the heart strikes chords of
inspiration
Synapsing the gap.
Allowing expression or not is our only choice
When the muse speaks.

Erotica

In silent innocence the game begins
Shyness fuels the fire
Igniting hidden passions lying in wait
Words not spoken hum in the air
Spinning threads that weave us together
Hand brushes arm
Eyes begin to glisten
Heartbeat cries to heartbeat
Drawing us to consummation as moths to
flame.

Another Day, Another Way

Growth stirs infinitude
Moment to moment perspective changes
Releasing the chains of judgment
As concepts of rightness and wrongness
dissolve in wisdom's light
The climb is gradual, for otherwise
Dizziness and confusion dominate.

For My Friend

As I was stumbling along in search of truth
Obsessed with a need to know Why?
You quietly entered my life.
Compelled to touch you, yet frightened and
shy
I awkwardly reached out and found you there
Slowly, unobtrusively (tho' not always)
We have been growing together
Sharing a little more each time
Building a bridge of trust that takes us to
safety.

Thank you.
I love you.

TRIUMPH

The Serpent of Denial

"Words drip from my mouth like honey
False nectar whose bitter-sweetness betrays,
belies, manipulates
Cloaked in love, disguising hate
I have no mercy for the helpless
The sting that conquers is intoxicating
Driving me to kill all who fall under my spell
Subtle poison."

Fatal Attraction

What is this Dance with Death
What glue binds this compulsion for abuse
When Love is offered I turn away, feeling
afraid.
When Love is withheld, conditional
I am consumed.
What is the power of darkness that seduces
one into oblivion?

The Quest

"I am only lovable when I am perfect,
therefore I am unlovable."

Redefining perfection
Shattering oppression
Releasing the human component from
judgment
Moving the guilt that hides Truth
All polarities must find resolution
In order that the
Divinity in Humanness
may at last be honored.

Helpless?

Those who kill seek death for themselves
Too angry for suicide, too undermined to
stop
They contaminate with their violence,
bleeding their pain
Silently screaming for help
Yet turning away when it is offered
Too lost in degradation to trust
How can we help?

Freedom

Covert intentionality twists, maims,
enshrouds truth
And ultimately enslaves.
Freedom requires the strength to unmask.

Synergy

Learning to accept love where it's found
Drinking in the golden nourishment
The Divine Gift allows the synergy of growth
to spark joy
Without question, without thought
Dancing flowers display their beauty for the
sun
Immutably bound, rejoicing in their
interdependency
Each feeds the other and all flourish.

Trust!

Two hearts touch
Shyly, hesitantly,
At first afraid of rejection
As courage grows
So does love.

UNBRIDLED JOY

Heart Dance

Birds in flight, love on the wing
Soaring, careening
Spinning patterns of joy that tickle the clouds
The waves leap gleefully
Splaying dappled, dancing diamonds
That glitter more sweetly
Because you are with me now.

Delight

Your energy precedes you
Celadon waves caress me gently
Bringing soft smiles that dapple my face
Thoughts of you sustain me
In most unusual ways.

Time for Love

I feel you entering my life
Distant thundering hooves that vibrate my
Heart
A herd of mustangs appear on the horizon of
my mind
Powerful, determined, free
It must be time for love.
I am ready.

Your Love

Your love is nourishing in ways that astonish
and delight
bringing starbursts of laughter and warmth
that light up my life.
your love is magic.

Your exquisite tenderness permeates my
Being
calling forth a wellspring of bliss that is
coloring my life beautiful.
Your love is healing.

Your unwavering integrity strengthens and
clarifies
acting like a beacon that guides us to safety.
Your love is trustworthy.

Your ingenuous nature has a light hand that
paints smiles and touches hearts
gifting others with flashes of joy.
Your love is beautiful.

Your compassionate concern for others is
apparent to all
igniting empathy and awakening aspirations
that open new avenues.
Your love is inspiring.

Your gentle sensitivity and receptive
awareness allow me to blossom in your eyes.
I see my own growth reflected there in quiet
acknowledgment and
ever-deepening appreciation.
Your love lets me Be who I Am.

Thank you for sharing your love.

Learning to Allow

Allowing love to enter in fully and touch all
corners of Being
requires strength, courage, fortitude
for love is relentless in its intent to heal
steadfastly stripping away falsity
layer after layer
.Bringing to light all aspects of self
Focusing uncomfortably on what we most
wish
to hide
So we may learn at last,
That even shadows and cobwebs
are lovable.

In Spiritu

When I'm in inspiration
Divine protection surrounds me
Cushioning softly
Refracting rainbow reflections scatter
joyously
Glittering up my soul.

When I'm in inspiration
Courage comes easy
Burdens dissolve into light
Senses are exaggerated yet refined
Every nuance registering
Ribboning through my consciousness
Wending and weaving into tapestries of gold.

When I'm in inspiration.

Terra Mother

I feel the cauldron of souls
Swirling, whirling dervishes struggling to be
free
If only you could learn that REALITY
nourishes
And surrender your defenses
Put down your weapons
Extend trust, if even for a moment
The universe is spanned with a handshake
Transformation begins with a spark.

Deepening

I ache for you tonight
I yearn for your sweet touch
Your teasing, gentle smile
I feel you in my heart, close in love
Yet, I ache for you tonight
Feeling other lovers' energies crisscrossing
between them
Brings you closer still
We have so far to go
I ache for you tonight.

HEART DANCE

The Drum Beats Louder Now

I dream of being in your arms
So much between us with so few words
So many seeming limitations
The current grows stronger, forging deeper,
ever deeper connections
Heart bonded to Heart
I feel our souls fusing in ecstatic rhythms that
ripple my body
Yet our lips have yet to meet.
The drum beats louder now
Growing in urgency.

It's All Up to Us

Within the confines of our universe
We have found eternity
When you are with me all separation
evaporates
Leaving sweet misty light that glows around
us
Creating the boundaries of our world.
It's all up to us.

Sorrow's River

My heart bleeds grief today
Long-buried wounds still too tender
Have revealed themselves at last
Sorrow's river washes me clean.

I Surrender

At last I am ready
For this final initiation
The ultimate obliteration of ego purpose
I surrender.

Alchemy

The force that constantly challenges
is wooed through agonies of respect and
humility.
Profound underpinnings that rule our lives
Must be exposed and shattered
Transmutation through essence and form.
Endless mirroring.
If not take mirth in process
'Twill be a boring journey indeed.

Journey to the Center

Deep blues and greens
My center, my self
untrammeled, wild
Lush rainforest dripping sensuality
Colors heighten awareness
To pristine rainbows that dazzle and quench
Here for basking in the rich, textural silence
That sings the strings of ecstasy
And brings blissful renewal.

Power is Nameless

Swooning in surrender
I confess the waves of my heart
Pound and arch sharply
Creating movement around me
Each one reflects his own definition to
consider
Power is nameless.

REBUILDING THE INFRASTRUCTURE

Dawn's Light

Braving the darkness brings us to claim our
untamable selves
In the wilderness of the soul
Pure power, raw yet refined
Swirling, whirling readiness
To be shaped and sculpted into the colors of
our lives
We hold it in our hands to create anything we
imagine.

The Wilderness of the Heart

The heart's wilderness holds all our records
Past, present, future
Skipping through fields of wonder
Over rocks of regret, skirting the abyss of
despair
Climbing trees of delight
Slivering through the darkness
The dankness of fear unclaimed
Skimming rocks on the shores of possibility
We find the endless frontier and rejoice.

The Untamed Heart

Untamed, unnamed, unveiled at last
The glory and adventure
Strength and courage
Relief and release
Of conquering the conqueror within
Who burns to control the uncontrollable
The hero who has lived for battle at last puts
down his weapons
To learn the secrets of the untamed heart.

I AM

I AM the endless ocean
The lapping serenity, the crashing obliterator
The breeze that caresses, the monsoon that
destroys
The fire that warms but also consumes
The earth that supports and nourishes
And without warning will engulf
I AM the silence surrounding song
The darkness that cradles all light
The current that carries the clouds
The space within a snowflake
Unseen, unseeable
Unknown, unknowable.
Untouched, untouchable
I AM the Source of All.
I AM the womb of man.

Innocence Reclaimed

Sparkling, dancing waters cleanse us
As we partake of the mysteries of each other
Tenderness and warmth lull us into
Sleepy twilight as we bask in afterglow
Nature's children, we revel in the fruits of
bodies shared
Openly, honestly, freely we play in laughter's
light
As romping beasts
No thought, no censure
Just pure and simple delight.

All-one-ness

Aloneness
Wholeness acknowledged
Energy contained, shared only with Self
Nourishes, cleanses, uplifts
Balanced with breezy exchanges
Solitude has its own brand of fulfillment.

Free At Last

Sorrow acknowledged is sorrow released
Dreams unachieved, carefully tended through
the years
Cry out for Death's peace.
Relief washes through us as we stand at the
shore
Silently watching the shattered pieces
Float out of sight.

GLORY

Heaven's Gate

At last, the struggle abates
Submission to fate's hand, rails against the
ego's drive to control
Broken and bloody, exhaustion overwhelms
Yet at heaven's gate, we stand in awe
Seared by illusions of terror and pain
Unwilling to trust
Until all else fails.

Birth

It is time to be born unto ourselves
To claim, each one the golden fruits
Of the Divinity Within.
The reign of darkness is over
Struggle's shackles are shattered
The vestiges of violence, terror's tyranny
Oppression's ignorance rule no more.
The last veils are lifted to reveal the splendor
Abundance and overflowing joy
That applaud our arrival in the glittering chambers
Of the Palace of an Untamed Heart.

Truth

Truth transmutes
The worst
Into Love.

Ignorance: The Voice of Death

If all the rage and all the hatred in the world
Were consolidated and turned against
Our solitary enemy of ignorance
Peace would blossom in an hour.

A New World Awaits

Armageddon destroys only itself
Awash in the waterfall, we rejoice
As the labor pains begin
Midwives of compassion await with
anticipation
Praying for an easy delivery.

The Crystal Chamber

The crystal chamber asserts itself
Embracing the Earth, our mother
Our Body
Its gentle compassion cradles us
Rocking in the New Dawn.

No Difference

All contributions no matter the size are
equally valid.
For each is completely unique
And none can substitute for another.
All pieces must be brought to light
In order to perceive
the ever-expanding whole.

BLUE BEAUTY

To Begin

When will we be free to see each other
and ourselves in our totality?
Not merely as man or woman
but human and divine.
When can we release the enmity inside?
The rage, the bitter seed
that holds fast the illusion of separation
that lashes out at anything or one not
understood.
When will the need to label disappear?
It only serves to diminish
and lends a false sense of control to the ego.
Only ignorance tears down
what it cannot comprehend.

Love is the Healer

When the child cries out
The threat of abandonment grips in terror
and desperation overwhelms
Open the portals of love between
Self and self.
It is right for a child to cling when in need
Unable to articulate
All she craves is reassurance.

In Its Wake

Healing the victim releases the tyrant
Who at last reunite in love's light
The victim's true jailor is guilt
The tyrant's: fear
Which play out in endless projection
Until the victim's guilt is tapped
And released into positive expression
This alone, allows the fear to move into
ownership
Once felt and expressed
The Mystery of Life works its magic
Leaving only love in its wake.

Unmasked

The internal tyrant has been unmasked by
love
Her sister, the victim suddenly sees the
mirror clearly
And feels only compassion
Bringing them both courage
Determination and self-respect
That now carries them to freedom
Together they are empowered to consolidate
And discover the only enemy that exists
Is ignorance.

The Choice is Ours

Where do we focus our power?
Which voices dominate our lives?
The voices of Love or fear.
Of Acceptance or rejection
Of understanding or separation.
The choice is ours
for free will rules all without exception.
Wisdom chooses discernment.
Love chooses Love.
Listen only to that which touches deeply and
echoes in the heart.
If pain be called forth, remember compassion
If it be Love, remember Joy.

Breaking the Spell

Staying separate from the judgment in
compassion's flame
Requires unflagging vigilance and a conscious
renewal
Of commitment in every moment.
When the way is lost
Awareness guides our return
The light is lost so readily
Closing our eyes and returning to oblivion is
the great seduction
The alarm clock of love
Needs our willingness to hear
To break the spell of illusion.

Holding Integrity

Boundaries are such tricky things
In times of safety, sharing love
The guard comes down
But awareness need be constant for
In a twinkling of an eye
The energy shifts.

THE PRIESTESS

Goodbye Ego Entanglements

I'm sorry
I can't see you again
The dance we share turns too fast to pain
Quickly clouding over my heart
With yesterday's veils
Even words can no longer be shared
For you are too far away to hear
And I can tarry no longer in this futility.

Love Never Ends

Love never ends
Only changes expression
When two who were one again become two
Celebration is still in order
For death inevitably brings life anew.
The cycles and circles of existence never end
They come 'round to greater heights
And ever more meaningful depths
One love leads to the next
And the next, and the next
Until at last, love for the One blends into All.

Cherish the Gifts

Gifts of love
Gifts of light
Each one carries her own unique design
The grand puzzle that illuminates all
With its unfoldment.

Pathway of Beauty

growth has its own roadmap, its own
timetable
each element progresses uniquely
on its pathway of beauty
with its chosen challenge an ever-recurring
theme
that molds and shapes the raw materials
into the Perfect Idea of Itself
thus does coal require pressure to become the
diamond
an oyster's irritation produces the pearl
all seeds germinate in darkness
and must push upward to find Light and
fulfillment
so, too must God's children find their way
through ignorance and fear to discover
the jewel within.

GAIASOPHIA ARISES

www.ingramcontent.com/pod-product-compliance
Lightning Source LLC
LaVergne TN
LVHW011036200726
843509LV00011B/1289